AF151812

YOUR KNOWLEDGE HAS VALUE

- We will publish your bachelor's and master's thesis, essays and papers

- Your own eBook and book - sold worldwide in all relevant shops

- Earn money with each sale

Upload your text at www.GRIN.com
and publish for free

Viraj Chorghe

Reversible data hiding in encrypted images

GRIN Publishing

Bibliographic information published by the German National Library:

The German National Library lists this publication in the National Bibliography; detailed bibliographic data are available on the Internet at http://dnb.dnb.de .

Imprint:

Copyright © 2014 GRIN Verlag GmbH
Print and binding: Books on Demand GmbH, Norderstedt Germany
ISBN: 978-3-656-83760-2

GRIN - Your knowledge has value

Since its foundation in 1998, GRIN has specialized in publishing academic texts by students, college teachers and other academics as e-book and printed book. The website www.grin.com is an ideal platform for presenting term papers, final papers, scientific essays, dissertations and specialist books.

Visit us on the internet:

http://www.grin.com/

http://www.facebook.com/grincom

http://www.twitter.com/grin_com

REVERSIBLE DATA HIDING IN ENCRYPTED IMAGES

Viraj P. Chorghe

Computer Engineering: Rajiv Gandhi Institute of Technology
Andheri(w),Mumbai, Maharashtra

Abstract: *This paper is a brief review in the field of Reversible data hiding in encrypted image. The protection of this multi-media data can be done with encryption or data hiding algorithms. Reversible data hiding (RDH) maintains the excellent property of the original image. Previous methods like embed data by reversibly vacating room from the encrypted images, which may subject to some errors on data extraction or in image restoration. With a traditional RDH algorithm, and thus it is easy for the data hider to reversibly embed data in the encrypted image. The proposed method can achieve real reversibility, i.e., data extraction and image recovery are free of any error.*

Keywords: **Reversible Data hiding, Image encryption, Histogram shift, PSNR.**

Introduction

In today's world, security is important aspect in day to day life. So, everyone used various ways for security purpose. People use passwords for their security. Digital images has increased rapidly on the Internet. Image security becomes increasingly important for many applications, e.g., confidential transmission, video surveillance, military and medical applications.

The protection of this multimedia data can be done with encryption or data hiding algorithms. in the encryption type , protection through encryption there are several methods to encrypt binary images or gray level images and second type the protection on digital watermarking or data hiding, aimed at secretly embedding a message into the data.

These two technologies can be used complementary and mutually commutative. These technique to encrypt an image for secure image transmission. In other approach the digital signature of the original image is added to the encoded version of the original image. The encoding of the image is done using an appropriate error control code. At the receiver end, after the decryption of the image, the digital signature can be used to verify the authenticity of the image. Encryption and watermarking algorithms also used.

Reversible data hiding techniques can be generally classified into two frameworks

- Vacate room after encryption

- Reserve room before encryption

In the first framework, vacate room after encryption (VRAE), a content owner first encrypts the original image using a standard cipher with an encryption key. After producing the encrypted image, the content owner hands over it to a data hider (e.g., a database manager) and the data hider can embed some auxiliary data into the encrypted image by losslessly vacating some room according to a data hiding key. Then a receiver, maybe the content owner himself or an authorized third party can extract the embedded data with the data hiding key and further recover the original image from encrypted version according to the encryption key.

In the second framework, reserve room before encryption (RRBE), the content owner first reserve enough space on original image and then converts the image into its encrypted version with the encryption key. Now, the data embed ding process in encrypted images is inherently reversible for the data hider only needs to accommodate data into the spare space previous emptied out. The data extraction and image recovery are identical to that of Framework VRAE. Obviously, standard RDH algorithms are the ideal operator for reserving room before encryption and can be easily applied to Framework RRBE to achieve better performance.

VRAE Methods

The methods "vacating room after encryption (VRAE)",is the one method we can use in the security . In this a content owner encrypts the original image using a standard cipher with an encryption key. After producing the encrypted image, the content owner hands over it to a data hider and the data hider can embed some auxiliary data into the encrypted image by losslessly vacating some room according to a data hiding key. Then a receiver may be the content owner himself or an authorized third party can extract the embedded data with the data hiding encrypted version according to the encryption key.

In other methods of the encrypted 8-bit gray scale images are generated by encrypting every bit planes with a stream cipher. The method in segments the encrypted image into a number of non-overlapping blocks sized by a×a, each block is used to carry one additional bit. To do this, pixels in each block are pseudo-randomly divided into two sets S1 and S2 according to a data hiding key. If the additional bit to be embedded is 0, flip the 3 LSBs of each encrypted pixel in S1, otherwise flip the 3 encrypted LSBs of pixels in S2.

For data extraction and image recovery, the receiver flips all the three LSBs of pixels in S1 to form a new decrypted block, and flips all the three LSBs of pixels in S2 to form another new block; one of them will be decrypted to the original block. Due to spatial correlation in natural images, original block is presumed to be much smoother than interfered block and embedded bit can be extracted correspondingly. However, there is a risk of defeat of bit extraction and image recovery when divided block is relatively small or has much fine-detailed textures.

Generation of Encrypted Image

For construct the encrypted image, the first stage can be divided into three steps: image partition, self-reversible embedding followed by image encryption. At the beginning, image partition step divides original image into two parts A and B; then, the LSBs of A are reversibly embedded into B with a standard RDH algorithm so that LSBs of A can be used for accommodating messages; at last, encrypt the rearranged image to generate its final version.

1) Image Partition
2) Self-Reversible Embedding
3) Image Encryption

1) Image Partition:

The goal of image partition is to construct a smoother area , on which standard RDH algorithms such as can achieve better performance. And achieve better security. To do that, without loss of generality, assume the original image is an 8 bits gray-scale image with its size M×N.

From the original image with the rows, some overlapping blocks having number is determined by the size of embedded messages, this will be denoted by "l". In detail, every block consists of m rows, where, m = [l/N] and the number of blocks can be computed through n= M-m+1. An important point here is that each block is overlapped by pervious and/or sub sequential blocks along the rows.

2) Self-Reversible Embedding

The goal of self-reversible embedding is to embed the LSB-planes of A into B by employing traditional RDH algorithms. For illustration, simplify the method in to demonstrate the process of self-embedding. But this will not apply in ant RDH algorithm.

Data can be embedded into the estimating error sequence with histogram shift. Estimating errors of black pixels Calculation done with the help of surrounding white. Then another estimating error sequence is generated which can accommodate messages and can also implement multilayer embedding scheme.

3) Image Encryption:
After the rearranged self-embedded image, denoted by X, will be generated. Then we have to encrypt X to construct the encrypted image, denoted by E .With a stream cipher, the encryption version of X is easily obtained. For example, a gray value ranging from 0 to 255 can be represented by 8 bits.

But after image encryption, the data hider or a third party cannot access the content of original image without the encryption key, thus privacy of the content owner being protected.

COMPARATIVE STUDY:

Sr no.	Title of paper	Year of publication	Methods used	Advantages/ disadvantages
1	Reversible data hiding	2006	Histogram modification, reversible data hiding, watermarking	Can embed more data with small distortion.
2	Reversible image watermarking using interpolation technique	2010	Additive interpolation error expansion, data hiding, interpolation error	High image quality without sacrificing embedding capacity.
3	Reversible data hiding in encrypted images	2011	Image encryption, image recovery, reversible data hiding	Low computation complexity. data can be extracted after decrypting the image
4	An improved data hiding in encrypted images using side match	2012	Encrypted image, reversible data hiding, side-match	Improved data extraction and image recovery, side match technique reduces error rate
5	Separable	2012	Image	Image

reversible data hiding in encrypted image		encryption, image recovery, reversible data hiding	recovery and data extraction can be performed in parallel.

Table 1

Data extraction and image recovery:

Since data extraction is completely independent from image decryption, the order of them implies two different practical applications.

1) Case 1: Extracting Data from Encrypted Images: To manage and update personal information of images which are encrypted for protecting clients' privacy, an inferior database manager may only get access to the data hiding key and have to manipulate data in encrypted domain. The order of data extraction before image decryption guarantees the feasibility of this work in this case. When the database manager gets the data hiding key, he can decrypt the LSB-planes of and extract the additional data by directly reading the decrypted version. When requesting for updating information of encrypted images, the database manager, then, updates information through LSB replacement and encrypts updated information according to the data hiding key all over again. As the whole process is entirely operated on encrypted domain, it avoids the leakage of original content.

2) Case 2: Extracting Data from Decrypted Images: In Case 1, both embedding and extraction of the data are manipulated in encrypted domain. On the other hand, there is a different situation that the user wants to decrypt the image first and extracts the data from the decrypted image when it is needed. The following example is an application for such scenario. Assume Alice outsourced her images to a cloud server, and the images are encrypted to protect their contents. Into the encrypted images, the cloud server marks the images by embedding some notation, including the identity of the images' owner, the identity of the cloud server and time stamps, to manage the encrypted images. Note that the cloud server has no right to do any permanent damage to the images. Now an authorized user, Bob who has been shared the encryption key and the data hiding key, downloaded and decrypted the images. Bob hoped to get marked decrypted

images, i.e., decrypted images still including the notation, which can be used to trace the source and history of the data. The order of image decryption before/without data extraction is perfectly suitable for this case.

CONCLUSION

RDE(Reversible data hiding in encrypted images) is a used because of the privacy-preserving requirements from cloud data management. Other methods implement RDH in encrypted images by vacating room after encryption, In thus the data hider can benefit it from the extra space emptied out in previous stage to make data hiding process effort-less. This method can take advantage of all old RDH techniques for plain images and achieve excellent performance without loss of perfect secrecy. Also method can achieve separate data extraction , greatly & real reversibility, improvement on the quality of marked decrypted images.

References

1. Ms.Fameela.K.A,Mrs. Najiya.A and Asst.prof.Mrs. Reshma.V.K," SURVEY ON REVERSIBLE DATA HIDING IN ENCRYPTED IMAGES", Department of Computer Science and Engineering, (IJSETR), Volume 3, Issue 4, April 2014

2. Wagh Mahesh J.1, Manish Koul, Murtadak Sona U., Shinde Kavita S., Prof. Bhandare M.G.," RDH(Reversible Data Hiding) in Encrypted Images by Reserving Room Before Encryption" Volume 4, Issue 4, April 2014.

3. Harish G, Smitha Shekar B, Prajwal R, Sunil S Shetty," Reversible Data Hiding In Encrypted Images by Reserving Room before Encryption" Department of Computer Science & Engineering, Dr. Ambedkar Institute of Technology, India. 01 July 2014